IMAGES
of America

ST. GEORGE

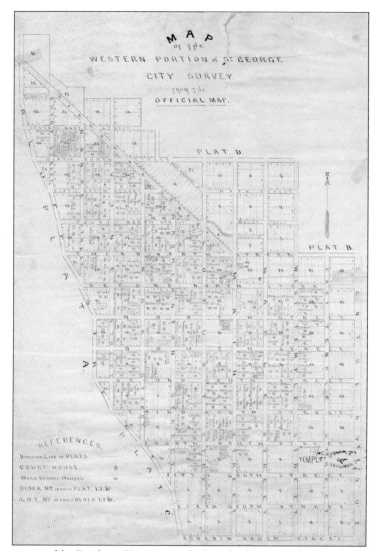

St. George was named by Brigham Young even before the location was selected. Just shy of two months after the arrival of the Southern Utah Mission settlers, the valley was surveyed, a spot was chosen, and lots were divided. On January 23, 1868, families began to move to their assigned lots. Before the town was plotted, the settlers set up tents at Encampment Mall, which today is in the heart of the Dixie State University campus. The section of town west of Main Street and north of 300 South Street was the first area developed. The move from the camp to the new town shifted the population a mile west and closer to sources of water. Three lots were set aside for schools, which many families donated funds to help build. This map is from a few decades later, but it shows many original family homes. (Courtesy of Special Collections & Archives at Dixie State University Library.)

ON THE COVER: St. George was carved out of a desert landscape, and despite the many obstacles the town faced in the early years, it has grown into a flourishing hub of recreation, tourism, and a thriving economy. The trailblazing spirit and strong work ethic of the early people have continued through the years. Local celebrations like parades and pageants connect the strength of the past with future growth. (Courtesy of Special Collections & Archives at Dixie State University Library.)

IMAGES
of America

ST. GEORGE

Kathleen Broeder and Dianne Aldrich

ARCADIA
PUBLISHING

Copyright © 2021 by Kathleen Broeder and Dianne Aldrich
ISBN 978-1-4671-0598-9

Published by Arcadia Publishing
Charleston, South Carolina

Printed in the United States of America

Library of Congress Control Number: 2020945374

For all general information, please contact Arcadia Publishing:
Telephone 843-853-2070
Fax 843-853-0044
E-mail sales@arcadiapublishing.com
For customer service and orders:
Toll-Free 1-888-313-2665

Visit us on the Internet at www.arcadiapublishing.com

*To our families who supported us,
to the Dixie State University Library that encouraged us,
and to the people who have loved St. George, we thank you.*

CONTENTS

Acknowledgments   6

Introduction   7

1.   Early People   11

2.   Social and Cultural Happenings   27

3.   Transforming from One-Room Schoolhouses   43

4.   The Business of Living   63

5.   Transformation from a Small Town   99

Bibliography   126

Index   127

ACKNOWLEDGMENTS

This book started with the simple idea of sharing with the world the amazing photographs found at the Special Collections & Archives in the Dixie State University Library. We extend our many thanks to the generations of St. George residents who gave their family papers and photographs to the archives. These donors demonstrated their loving commitment to St. George and local history by giving their remarkable stories for preservation and safekeeping for future generations to enjoy. It is our pleasure to share that same love of St. George's history with the world in this book. We especially want to thank the Special Collections & Archives staff, Tracey O'Kelly and Tammy Gentry, for their continuous support in retrieving materials.

This book would not have been possible without the mentorship of a terrific boss, dean of library and learning services Kelly Peterson-Fairchild, who encourages us to push our boundaries.

We also wish to thank all those at Arcadia Publishing for their many efforts—especially Artie Crisp for sticking with us until we were ready to get started and Angel Hisnanick for her positive encouragement and patience.

Most especially, we would like to thank our husbands. You know who you are and exactly what you did to help us get this book finished. Our children gave us all their love and quiet strength. We hope to make them proud. We owe our gratitude to our parents, who inspired us to set our goals high and gave us the courage to see our dreams through to the end. Lucy and Rusty gave us puppy love and made everything better.

Lastly, I would like to thank my co-author, who, somewhere in the middle of this process, became a best friend, my wedding officiant, and the best co-worker a gal could ever have.

Unless otherwise noted, all images are courtesy of Special Collections & Archives at Dixie State University Library.

INTRODUCTION

The boundaries of what locals refer to as "Utah's Dixie" are ill-defined. All would agree that it encompasses Washington County. While some might narrow it down to just St. George, others expand it to include the Arizona Strip and Nevada's northeast corner. Perhaps James Bleak was correct in believing that the towns that preceded the 1861 settlement of St. George are inextricably connected and part of Southern Utah's story. He could not tell the story of the colonization, growth, and development of St. George without recounting previous events.

William Fawcett and Robert Thompson first arrived in the valley that became known as St. George on November 25, 1861, as part of an advance party of the Southern Utah Mission. The rest of their group, over 309 families, followed six days later, and the largest Latter-Day Saint (LDS) colony in Washington County began. It is easy to mistake the 1861 Mormon pioneers who settled St. George with the first history of Southern Utah. While it is true that it marked the first consistent written recording of events, thanks in large part to James Bleak's *Annals of the Southern Mission*, the Mormon pioneers by no means entered an unpopulated area. There was already a robust Mormon presence and several bands of Southern Paiutes.

Earlier, during the first meetings between local tribes and the Mormon missionaries called to convert the Southern Paiutes in June 1854, Bleak recorded the initial fear the various bands exhibited. He attributes their fear to previous raids made by Mexicans and Utes who sold stolen children into slavery in California. After the first moments of fear, friendly relations developed, and missionaries learned about their new neighbors, baptized 11 Native American people who lived near the Santa Clara River, and even saw a miracle of healing for a woman after tribal medicine failed. Bleak also commented on the Shivwits band of Southern Paiutes farming wheat, corn, squash, and melons. As part of this initial contact, the missionaries told them of the "big captain," Brigham Young, who said that one day, whites would come live among the Paiutes. Seven years later, the 309 families arrived to fulfill the Southern Utah Mission.

Over a dozen Mormon colonies were already established by 1861, including Fort Harmony (1852); Santa Clara (1854); Hamblin and Pinto (1856); Gunlock, Virgin, and Washington (1857); Heberville, Pintura, and Toquerville (1858); Grafton, Harrisburg, and Pine Valley (1859); and Adventure (1860). Many of these colonies were created as forts for Indian missionaries, while other towns only consisted of a few family farms. The settlements were small and struggled to survive. Some quickly became ghost towns, whose skeletal remains can still be visited. Several survive today as small towns, and others have become part of the larger St. George metropolitan area.

The history before 1861, when the LDS pioneers entered St. George, can be tricky to track through written records. Names of places and rivers changed through the first half of the 19th century and only solidified after colonization. Bits and pieces from early white exploration can be collected. The land the pioneers traveled through and settled was not empty. As early as 1776, while the area was part of Mexico, Dominguez and Escalante made their famous trek from Santa Fe to find a path to California to join two outposts of the Spanish empire. Between mid-October to mid-November, the expedition traveled south through Kanarraville, Toquerville, Hurricane, and then down into the Arizona Strip until they finally emerged at Lee's Ferry. From there, they continued to Santa Fe. During their travels, the expedition relied on the many Native Americans from the various bands they met for directions to the Colorado River, to find water, and replenish their food supplies. The portion of their journey between Hurricane and Lee's Ferry was a period of extreme hunger, thirst, and mistrust of local tribes. As their condition worsened, there was more preaching of Christianity to local tribes. Their interactions with the Native Americans were quite telling of both the locals' and the expedition members' thoughts and feelings.

As the Dominguez-Escalante Expedition headed south through Kanarraville, they met a small group of Native Americans. The wary native men agreed to guide the expedition south out of their lands to Ash Creek Canyon, near Pintura, where they quickly vanished and left the group to find its own way. Between Toquerville and Hurricane, the expedition came across three maize fields with well-dug irrigation ditches. The evidence of farming overjoyed the expedition for two reasons. First, it gave them hope of finding provisions. Second, it indicated a more developed society that would more easily lead the local natives to be converted to "civil ways of living and to the faith whenever the Most High so disposes." Next, the expedition passed by the hot springs in the Virgin River (which they named Rio de las Piramides Sulfurosas due to the sulfur scent) between Hurricane and LaVerkin.

As they headed south, the expedition followed recent Native Americans tracks to low sandy places where their mounts became exhausted. They encountered eight Mojave men, who offered to trade turquoise beads. During the ensuing conversation, the Mojave men warned that, in two days, they would reach the Colorado River and that the Grand Canyon would block their passage. The Mojave insisted they could not continue south. Still, the expedition members were unwilling to trust them, in case they were purposefully misled due to politics between bands. The expedition was out of food and water. In searching through all their luggage, they only found a bit of brown sugarloaf and a few pieces of squash some servants had secretly obtained from some Shivwits men. Two days later, they came across another small group of Native American men who, after much persuasion, agreed to guide them to water, near today's Bobcat Reservoir in the Arizona Strip. They were also able to trade for supplies and get a new set of instructions for reaching the Colorado River. As they made their way toward the ford at what is now Lee's Ferry, the expedition camped with a group of Kaibab Paiutes, who sold them food and performed a healing ritual for one of the expedition members. Once the healing ceremony was explained to the expedition leaders, Escalante strongly chastised the Kaibab and instructed them in the Christian doctrine. Escalante took issue with the Native Americans for refusing to sell meat. Instead, the Kaibab were only willing to sell wild plants that made expedition members ill. As the expedition traveled, they had a difficult time finding the ford on their own. Eventually, they were successful in crossing the Colorado River and returning to Santa Fe. While the expedition never made it to California, a portion of the trail they traveled became part of the Old Spanish Trail.

The tale of Southern Utah between the early 1820s and late 1840s is incomplete without mention of Mexico, which became independent of Spain in the early 1820s. Under Mexican rule, the Spanish Trail leading to the Pacific became a regular commercial route. Southern Utah was explored and described by fur trapper Jedediah Smith in 1826–1827 as he searched for a route from the Great Salt Lake to Southern California. Smith was one of the few fur trappers to record his explorations in a journal. The names of places and peoples were not yet formally recognized when Smith wrote his account. He traveled down the Santa Clara River (Corn Creek), where he met Native Americans (Pa-Ulches) who raised corn and pumpkins. In 1826, Smith went down the Virgin River (Adams River) through the narrow cut in the Beaver Dam Mountains. His path followed today's Interstate 15 route through the Virgin River Gorge and into the Muddy River area of Nevada. In 1827, Smith traveled an alternate course through Santa Clara and over Utah Hill, later followed by Highway 91. Smith helped open the Old Spanish Trail to California for future travelers, and it led straight through the heart of Washington County.

The Old Spanish Trail is the most arduous pack mule route in the history of the United States, at over 1,200 miles. Traders and their mule trains usually traveled the trail once a year in round trips between Santa Fe and Los Angeles through mostly barren and sparsely populated lands. The peak use of the trail was in the 1830s and 1840s when the area was part of Mexico. Well into the 1850s and 1860s, after the Mexican-American War when the territory was ceded to the United States, the portion of the trail through Southern Utah remained in use by overland pioneers traveling from the eastern states to California. Mountain Meadows, near Pine Valley and Pinto, was a popular camping site on the trail for immigrant wagon trains. When Mormon pioneers began exploring and settling the remote area of St. George, it became the most populated location for hundreds of miles around. Mountain Meadows became a welcome break from the isolation of much of the Old Spanish Trail. Little did they know that this beautiful camping site would become a place of tragedy when a wagon train of Arkansas immigrants was massacred by Mormons from the nearby towns in 1857. The attack was fueled in part by fear and hysteria over the Utah War.

St. George relied on trade with Salt Lake City and the wagon trains to grow and develop. The first few backbreaking decades of growth were marked with recurring flooding and deprivation. To survive, St. George and the surrounding towns needed to work together. James Bleak had to recount the history of the existing towns in Washington County before he could journal the events of the new town of St. George as they unfolded. The story of St. George cannot be told in isolation.

The written local history records available in the Dixie State University Library Special Collections & Archives afford historians a unique view into the past. The many photographs found there help to bring those words to life. The advent of the camera created an entirely new medium to share memories of events. Throughout the rest of this book, images and written records have been combined to share memories of the early people and the work they did to build the foundations of our community in St. George.

One

EARLY PEOPLE

Beloved Southland, dear to me
My Dixie Home, My Dixie Home
My heart in song I raise to thee
My Dixie Home! My Dixie Home!
Land where my fathers toiled and died,
Once scorned of men, but now their pride
I'll sing thy praises far and wide,
My Dixie Home! My Dixie Home!

—Anthony W. Ivins

The prosperity of St. George was won from the desert through toil, grit, and perseverance. Early Mormon settlers sent to cultivate the land struggled in a barren and remote desert. The Virgin River flooded yearly and was very difficult to tame. Ironically, even though there were moments of too much water coming from the river, there was also a pervasive shortage of good drinking water. Food was also short in the early years, which was made worse by the emphasis on growing cotton rather than food crops. These shortages, combined with widespread illness, intense heat, very alkaline soil (which was terrible for growing crops), and the remoteness, gave a very thin margin of safety against ruin. Yet they persisted and overcame.

Even after the town was secure, life continued to be complicated. For many, the Great Depression in the 1930s had little effect on their daily lives because they were already struggling. It just made a hard life a bit harder. The remarkable thing about St. George was the close-knit community and its drive to succeed. While it took the whole community to survive, here are a few selected individuals and their stories.

A year after the famous Dominguez-Escalante Expedition sought a route from Santa Fe to California, the expedition's cartographer, Bernardo de Miera y Pacheco, created this map charting their course. The expedition never made it to California. Instead, they traveled a circuitous route from Santa Fe north to Utah Lake, south through Washington County, along the Arizona Strip, and across the Colorado River at Lee's Ferry before heading back to Santa Fe. Many of the Spanish place names are still recognizable, such as Lago Timpanogos (Utah Lake). Others, like the Rio de las Piramides Sulfurosas (Virgin River) are much more difficult to connect. It is even harder to make sense of the landmarks and directions. The portion of the route through Washington County is at lower left. (Courtesy of the Library of Congress, Geography and Map Division.)

In the 1851 LDS Conference, Brigham Young originally intended for the first Mormon settlement in Washington County to be where St. George is now located. Young called John D. Lee (pictured) to start a settlement where the Santa Clara and Virgin Rivers met. Instead, Lee built Fort Harmony, the first permanent town near the northern border of Washington County.

Taufe von Qui-tuß und 130 anderen Indianern des Shebit-Stammes durch Mormonen-Missionäre, in St. George, Utah. (S. 366.)

In March 1875, Qui-Tuss, a respected chief of the Shivwits band of Southern Paiutes, was baptized by Daniel McArthur in a pond just north of St. George along with approximately 150 Shivwits men, women, and children. The baptism was photographed as an example of the white man's conquest of the West and the conversion of the native inhabitants to civilized religion. It was reproduced internationally as a lithograph, as seen here.

Hannah Maria Woodbury was born in 1834 in Salem, Massachusetts. She married Thales Haskell in 1855, who served in the dangerous Southern Utah Indian Mission. Unfortunately, on June 23, 1857, she and her unborn baby died due to an accidental gunshot. A young adopted Native American boy picked up a gun off a shelf, and it accidentally discharged.

Jacob Hamblin maintained his home with several wives on the Santa Clara River between 1863 and 1868 while serving in the Southern Utah Indian Mission. He was called to the mission in 1854 to work with and convert local Native Americans. After most of the fort in Santa Clara washed away, he built his home, which served as the headquarters of the mission.

THE SCENE OF THE MOUNTAIN MEADOWS MASSACRE, UTAH TERRITORY.—[From a recent Sketch.]

Mountain Meadows was a camping and grazing site on the Old Spanish Trail used by travelers heading to California. Just four years before the Southern Utah Mission, federal troops marched toward Utah to put down a rebellion. War hysteria spread rapidly among Mormons as Brigham Young prepared the militia to stand against the troops in a conflict known as the Utah War. Mormons could vividly recall previous persecutions in the East and vowed never to submit again. In September 1857, the non-Mormon Baker-Fancher parties from Arkansas, except for 17 children, were massacred by Mormons and Native Americans. It was the most horrific moment in an otherwise bloodless war. Mormon involvement in the massacre was a closely held secret, and blame was shifted to the Native Americans, so those responsible could avoid prosecution. Only one man, John D. Lee, was held accountable for the crime of many and executed at Mountain Meadows a full 20 years after the massacre.

SAINSBURY AND JOHNSON.

S&J

SALT LAKE CITY, UTAH.

James Bleak was set apart by church leaders to be clerk and historian for the new Southern Utah Mission. In his *Annals of the Southern Mission*, Bleak recorded detailed accounts of the early creation of St. George. For instance, immediately after arriving in the valley in November 1861, the mission sought to use the Virgin River for irrigation and picked a site for the new town. Bleak actively served in the Sunday school, as city recorder, as a counselor in the bishopric, stake presidency, and high council. He was responsible for the first tithing office in a little adobe building. In 1871, Brigham Young called Bleak on a mission to Europe to give him a much-needed rest because he was working too hard. Bleak also was passionate about education. He taught Spanish classes for several years, was one of the first to incorporate a library, and served on the board of the first and second iterations of the St. George Stake Academy.

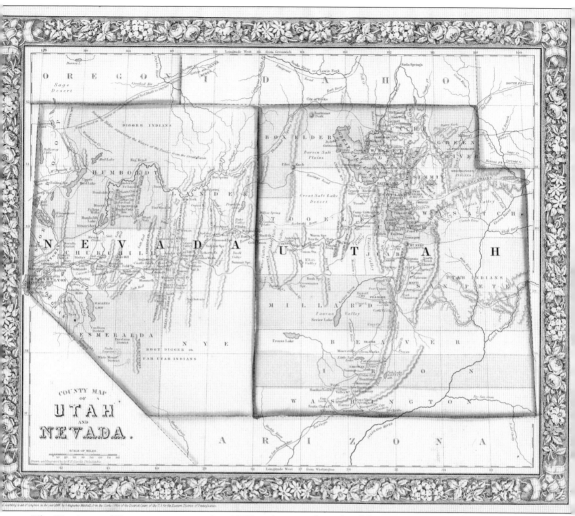

The Territory of Deseret was created in 1850 and covered much of the present states of Nevada and Utah along with part of Colorado. In 1861, Nevada was carved from the territory, which reduced Utah's size. Over the next seven years, big pieces of Utah Territory were parceled out to Colorado, Wyoming, and Idaho until Utah resembled its current size. Final boundaries were set in 1892, and the territory became a state in 1896. In this 1865 map, Washington County encompassed the entire southern portion of the territory from just west of St. George and east to where Blanding is today. Some cities like St. George, Santa Clara, Washington, Tocqueville, Virgin, Pine Valley, Kanarra, and New Harmony are still on today's maps. Other towns like Adventure, Grafton, Grape Vine Springs, Harrisville, Hamlins Ranch, and Old Harmony live only in memory.

17

Born in 1847, Robert C. Lund was St. George's first telegraph operator. Later, he became a partner in Woolley, Lund, and Judd mercantile stores in St. George and Silver Reef, providing competition for the St. George Co-Operative Store founded by Erastus Snow. He served as mayor and coroner of St. George, a missionary, and state representative for equal education.

As children of the original pioneers, David Morris and his wife, Annabella, settled and spent their lives in their home at 158 North Main Street. Morris was a lawyer, and in 1908 began his civic career serving in local and state governments. He served as a district judge and a Democratic member of Utah's House of Representatives during World War I. He valued education and co-founded St. George Stake Academy.

It was common during the 1800s for Mormon pioneers in Utah to trade or purchase Native American children from local tribes. Many children were adopted into Mormon homes, while others were typically indentured to work for the family for 20 years. The C.J. Arthur family adopted Sam in 1856, pictured here with their biological son Christopher "Tiffer" Arthur. At least three other Native American children were bought and traded in St. George's early years. Jacob Hamblin's brother offered a newly arrived family a Native American girl for $50. The mother had always wanted a girl and begged her husband to buy her. Another young Native American girl was taken into the home of James Keate. They named her Cora, and one of his wives, "Auntie" Keate, taught Cora to read and do figures. A Mr. Stevens near Springdale bought a two-year-old Native American boy from some Utes. He in turn sold the child to James Lemmon for a black horse. The child's name was changed to David, and he was raised as part of the household.

Around 1890, the young men and ladies of the Mutual Improvement Association in St. George included Brother MacFarlane, James Andrus, Anthony Ivins, Brother Thompson, Brother Miles, and Artemesia Snow. They met to continue their training in the "path of righteousness." Pres. George Q. Cannon said in 1899 that "the future of the people depends upon the training and education of the young."

Issac Riddle was looking for his lost cow when he stumbled upon Pine Valley. As early as 1856, Pine Valley was essential in supplying lumber to surrounding areas, even in the construction of the St. George Temple. The Pine Valley Chapel was completed in 1873 using local timber and has been in continual use as a church ever since, making it one of the oldest LDS churches still in service.

Faithful LDS church members paid their tithing with whatever they could. Everything from fruits and vegetables to livestock was accepted. By necessity, the tithing office became a storehouse. Tithing scrip was used to pay for labor at church construction sites, like the temple and tabernacle, and could be redeemed at the tithing office for food and other goods. A custom during the Christmas season was to open the tithing office to in-need Native Americans camping near the adobe brickyard in St. George. Members of the Shivwits, Navajo, and Ute tribes would travel to partake of the beans, potatoes, butter, eggs, beef, and other items the bishopric handed out from the storehouse provided by church members. In November 1902, Carl Weeks visited St. George for his health and took this photograph of Jim Moenich and Simon Loeb at the tithing office.

Nearly 60 years after St. George was first settled, the remaining settlers from 1861 were celebrated as pioneers in the 1930s. As children in the Southern Utah Mission, they struggled through the heat, inadequate water, and isolation to build a community in an inhospitable and sterile land. Although just children, they worked alongside their families and deserved to be recognized as pioneers who helped to build St. George.

In this photograph, Gus Hardy poses in front of his grandfather Augustus P. Hardy's 1854 rock etching. The elder Hardy was one of the first men to settle Fort Harmony and later Santa Clara with Jacob Hamblin. While seeking supplies in Parowan, Hardy brought back the first cotton seed to the area. Just behind his home, which still stands in Ancestor Square, Hardy built a small jail during his term as sheriff between 1877 and 1883.

Donald McGregor left Utah for medical school in 1899 and returned in 1903 as a surgeon. During his early years as a doctor, he was often frustrated with performing operations on a kitchen table with poor lighting and no trained assistance. In 1913, he converted a boarding house to his new workspace, the Washington County Hospital, better known as the McGregor Hospital, at 100 East and Tabernacle Streets. It was the only hospital in Utah south of Salt Lake City and had two full operating rooms. Despite living in a rural town, Dr. McGregor maintained his surgical skills by attending national conferences. The local newspaper routinely reported on surgery patients at the hospital, where McGregor treated everything from trauma patients to people recovering from pneumonia. Seen here on Armistice Day 1938, Dr. McGregor drives a wagon in the town parade, just as he had as a young doctor.

Victories are sweet, but not the ultimate goal. Instead, clean, wholesome association and sportsmanship were the goals of the Woodward Schools' sports teams in 1932. It was an especially important message as students from the Shivwits Reservation attended Woodward School for the first time. The Native American students were formed into a separate team.

During the 1930s, Mary Phoenix was a student body officer at Dixie Junior College. Phoenix never wanted to be a stereotypical housewife. Even after marriage, she succeeded in defying that stereotype. She co-chaired the Southern Utah War Bond Committee during World War II, chaired the Democratic Party, wrote local pageants, was a beloved high school English teacher, and perhaps was best remembered for her weekly column "Dixie Diary" in the local newspaper.

Mary Hafen Leavitt (first row, second from right) raised a large family in a one-room adobe house in Bunkerville on the Arizona Strip in the late 1800s through the early 1900s. Her daughter Juanita Pulsipher Brooks (first row, far right) developed a love for history and is most well-known for her honest and enlightening research on the Mountain Meadows Massacre. As a young woman and a widow, she attended college while raising a small child. After graduation, she served as English faculty at Dixie Junior College from 1925 to 1933. From 1928 to 1929, she took a sabbatical from teaching to earn her masters' degree at Columbia University. When she returned to St. George, she served as dean of women at Dixie Junior College. Brooks often took the overnight bus to the Huntington Library to use research materials while writing her books and articles about Southern Utah's history.

Maurine Whipple is remembered as the author of *The Giant Joshua*, a bestselling fictionalized story of early St. George life and polygamy. She won the Houghton Mifflin literary fellowship for the story of a young woman who became the third wife of a prominent St. George man. This third wife fell in love with her husband's oldest son, who was near her own age. The story ends in tragedy. For many locals, it was easy to connect actual families to the characters. A national reviewer wrote, "It is everything you want in a novel; it is thrilling frontier saga; it is an understanding picture of Mormon life; it is a portrait gallery of Mormon leaders in all their shrewdness, their force and their courage." Whipple intended for her book to be the first installment in a trilogy. She wrote a Utah travel guide book in 1945, but *The Giant Joshua* remained her only novel.

Two

SOCIAL AND CULTURAL HAPPENINGS

In fewer years than one would guess, ward halls were underway,
To serve for Church on Sundays, and for school on each weekday.
Ward Concerts, parties, dances, and events were also held there,
And the Old Social Hall was used for every "Grand Affair."
But the halls in these four centers of this little Mormon town,
Served a great and mighty purpose in those days, and gained renown,
As the school where sons and daughters of those Pioneers received.
The early training, fitting them of goals which they achieved.

—Mabel Jarvis
May 1937

Social events such as dances, parades, theater, music, and arts were the key ingredients of St. George's success. Mormon communities like St. George are built with homes together in villages and the farms on the outskirts of town. This configuration was purposeful and helpful in creating a strong sense of community. The many calls to settle Washington County brought people from all over the world. What they faced was barren land, far from everything they had known and loved. The one thing early settlers had in common was a commitment to their religion. Church leaders promoted social events to combat the frustrations that could easily defeat such a remote settlement.

The dedication to social events is evidenced by St. George Hall, which was the first building finished in St. George, just two years after pioneers arrived. The hall was built before the tabernacle, temple, or even ward houses. It and the Social Hall were used for five decades as the center of a thriving social community. Outside of the halls, the community came together with picnics and church outings. As St. George grew and aged, social events and the arts remained central to its sense of community.

Mail and social interactions were crucial to the wellbeing of the early inhabitants of St. George. A handful of days after arriving in 1861, the town collectively asked for a weekly mail service to replace the 12-to-20-day mail route between Salt Lake City and the Southern Utah Mission. A month after the plea for more efficient mail service, Erastus Snow suggested erecting a social and educational stone building during a camp meeting. Almost half of the new families each pledged $10 to $50 and nearly raised the building's full cost before any of them had homes or a roof over their heads. This image features a post office in the late 1800s next to the F&S General Merchandise Store, which occupied the original St. George Hall on Main Street and St. George Boulevard, completed in 1865. After the Social Hall was built in 1880, the original St. George Hall was sold to private enterprises.

Built on top of the cellar previously used to process wine for sacrament, the Social Hall was completed in 1880. The new Social Hall at the corner of Main and 200 North Streets replaced the original St. George Hall and quickly became the center of cultural events in town. Dances, plays, and mini-operas were performed regularly to bring culture and joy to the community. The floor was built to move into a sloping position so the audience could see from any of the seats, or it could be moved into a flat position for parties and dances. Tickets cost between 50¢ and 75¢, and most attendees paid with produce rather than money, which was scarce. From about 1920 to 1940, so many operas and vaudeville shows were performed that the Social Hall was referred to as the "opera house."

St. George was lucky to have James J. Booth, a local photographer with a studio. By 1896, Booth had expanded into a thriving mercantile business as well. Pictured here are Frank Bleak (left) and Joseph Snow, dressed in Scottish attire, possibly for a production of Sir Walter Scott's *Rob Roy*. The two would later become brothers-in-law when Joseph married Frank's sister Olive Thompson Bleak.

Sunday school and other church-related auxiliaries gave the youth a sense of community by hosting dances, parties, and candy pulls. The local Sunday school officers and teachers, pictured in 1897 in front of the tabernacle, prepared the lessons and activities central to childhood in St. George. At least one teacher around this time gave the advice, "Girls, don't get the sweet rubbed off."

During the 1912–1913 school year, the first operetta performance of the St. George Stake Academy was *Billee Taylor*. Directed by Joseph McAllister, it was a comedy of love, betrayal, and cross-dressing lady sailors. Much of the reported success of the operetta was attributed to McAllister's direction. Gordon Riding played the lead role and received accolades.

During World War I, a group of St. George women heeded the Red Cross's call for help. They pledged their support, "yes we will knit." These women met weekly to sew, knit, and do their bit. After the war ended, they formed the Athena Club, named for the goddess of home and marriage. Together, these women discussed current events, reviewed literature, played games, and hosted parties for several decades.

In 1917, the United States entered World War I and started drafting young men from around the country. At least 68 young men from Washington County served in the war, and there were 14 casualties, approximately a 20-percent fatality rate. St. George hosted military drills and parades at the town center with the residents there as support. Since about 85 percent of soldiers from the county had been or were current students of Dixie Academy, the 1918 yearbook is full of tributes to their soldiers and the war effort. In it, the student body wanted the soldiers from the college to know, " 'Equality of humanity' is your cause, the 'Dixie' is your home, the world is your nation and we are with you." No matter how remote or small (approximately 2,000 people) the community of St. George was, the world sometimes intruded violently.

Father Time— "Make the most of what remains."

The end of World War I on Armistice Day, November 11, 1918, brought peace to the world, but troubles still abounded with Spanish influenza. To help reduce the spread of the flu, Dixie Normal College closed its doors in late October for the remainder of the semester. St. George was warned to keep children at home, limit unnecessary visiting, and avoid gatherings. Masks were required by law to be worn in public. Dixie students gave a mask fashion show when the college reopened. One student, Jessie Hunt, died from pneumonia after catching influenza while the school was closed. Spanish influenza continued for almost two years. In 1920, it was reported to be spreading like wildfire. The ill were quarantined, and deaths continued. That year even the college president, Erastus Snow Romney, died from influenza compilations.

School and community events were inextricably intertwined in St. George. The Dixie Normal College sought ways to serve its community beyond its hometown. "He who would be master first must serve," was an old adage the music department had in mind when it put on the opera *Boccaccio* in 1921. The performers traveled to all the main towns in Southern Utah, including

Hurricane, Cedar City, Parowan, Enterprise, and St. George at the Opera House. The newspaper reported it as an event not to be missed. The opera was a widely celebrated success, with excellent leading characters, orchestra, and direction from Prof. Joseph McAllister.

By 1929, half of all Americans owned a car and were spending more money and time on leisure activities such as vacations. For many in Southern Utah, camping was the perfect escape. A trip to Pine Valley was made more comfortable with a vehicle. It also let campers escape the heat of summer in a time before air conditioning.

Dixie Junior College's freshman class commemorates the Great Depression with a parade banner that reads "1933-35 Poverty" as they march past the Big Hand Cafe and Whiteway Ice Cream. One young man recalled, "It was bad around St. George. We could not find any work to do." Another recalled his inability to pay his ninth-grade tuition of $10 and not being able to continue school.

One of Pres. Franklin D. Roosevelt's responses to the Great Depression was the Civilian Conservation Corps (CCC), which hired young men. From November 1933 to May 1934, the Washington CCC camp PE-216 was housed in front of the old cotton mill, which they used for storage, a smithy, and a garage. The CCC boys built a dam and diversion canal above Washington and jetties in the Virgin River to control flooding.

There were over 15 CCC camps in Washington County. The St. George Camp, north of Diagonal Street and east of Bluff Street, housed several units of men who worked on various water conservation and grazing projects. The biggest accomplishment was controlling the flooding of the Santa Clara River with re-silting plans and the Winsor (Shem) Dam in the Shivwits Reservation, which was completed in March 1935.

St. George may have been a sleepy town, but just like the rest of the country, it started seeing better days as the United States prepared for World War II. Two young ladies, Arvilla and Marie, stand in front of two billboards; one for electricity and the other for the movie *His Girl Friday*, a screwball comedy starring Cary Grant and Rosalind Russell. The film played in the Gaiety Theater at 68 East Tabernacle Street for three days in January 1940. When the movie theater was first built in 1911, it was called the Electric Theater and seated 220 moviegoers. A change in ownership in 1930 led to it being renamed the Gaiety. The theater showed movies for 88 years. It is still in use today as a city cultural hall with plays, lectures, and other performance events held regularly.

Centinial St George Ut. No 15. Year 1947.
R.D. Adams Photo.

Utah celebrated the 100th anniversary of Mormons entering Utah with art, music, and dance. In St. George, a week-long celebration ended with a pageant on the St. George temple grounds. "The Spirit of Dixie," written by Mabel Jarvis, told the story of the growth of St. George. The pageant was so well received that a second performance was held. In all, about 5,000 attendees enjoyed the pageant.

A fine-arts festival was held in late February 1949 with an exhibit from local artists. It is quite likely that these two diligent artists from Dixie Junior College contributed a traditional landscape and an expressionist vampire. Early that same year, a guest lecturer revealed the importance of art: "Pictures are more than mirrors of nature—they reveal what the artist sees; they reveal his individuality."

In the spring annual dance revue of 1951, about 80 Dixie students performed 20 dances, showing off their talent and grace. Drums accompanied a dance between Tarzan and Jane. Mexican, Russian, and Swiss numbers were included, along with the four seasons and "The Spirit of Dixie" dances. One dance included a blackface minstrel show.

Homecoming has always been a special time in St. George. In 1973, actress Ginger Rogers had the honor of being the grand marshal of the "The Happy Times"–themed homecoming parade. To Rogers, the homecoming events were "beautiful and enchanting." The parade traveled along Main Street. This picture was taken close to the corner at Tabernacle Street and shows Snow's Furniture and Snow's Dress Shop in the background.

St. George gets more than 300 days of sunshine each year, lending itself to outdoor activities. Skateboarding made a resurgence in the 1970s and was a hit with the youth. To support this physical activity, St. George Parks and Recreation held skateboarding competitions and put in a skateboarding park. This skateboarder is showing off his skills in a half-pipe set up near the tabernacle.

Officially named the Starlite Drive-In, this outdoor movie theater was also known as the Dixie Auto-Vue. The drive-in was a popular spot for all ages to watch films during the summer months from their vehicles. The outdoor theater offered residents and visitors the opportunity to view popular movies that had been distributed nationwide. Originally opening in 1949, the first motion pictures shown at the theater were *India Speaks* and *Ringside*.

As early as 1915, St. George had a skating rink, movie theater, dance hall, and bowling alley to entertain the community. In 1940, the St. George Bowling Alley opened for business. Everyone was invited to bowl for their health, but drinking and off-color language were prohibited, making it a welcoming environment for women. James "Jimmy" Stewart (center) took a break from filming to hit a few pins at the alley and mingle with friends and locals. Even though Stewart was a devout Presbyterian, he felt a deep connection to Utah and the strong Mormon values that were shared by the majority of the population. This connection was so strong that Stewart donated his correspondence, films, and scripts to one of the large Utah universities. These days, St. George has three bowling alleys that provide air conditioning, making bowling a great activity during the heat of the summer.

Three

TRANSFORMING FROM ONE-ROOM SCHOOLHOUSES

The history of school buildings, though within our comprehension,
Has a score or so of points that deserve more frequent mention,
And there's nothing give more pleasure, than now and then to trace,
The forward march of Pioneers who settled in this place.
While most of them lacked schooling, save by 'Hard Knock's heavy rule,
They planned that their descendants might know the joy of school;
And as soon as they were settled in St. George's first rude camp
At the 'dobe yard, the Cannon Tent held education's lamp.
'Twas nothing but a tallow dip, compared with schools today,
But it served to tell the people that real schools were on their way.
And the boys and girls who entered that tent school in '61
Have descendants here who understand how well their work was done.

—Mabel Jarvis
May 1937

Education and literacy have always been valued in St. George. Before the Southern Utah Mission was called in 1861, schools and school boards were already in evidence in Fort Harmony, Santa Clara, Washington City, Pine Valley, and Toquerville. It required toil to subdue the wilderness, and sometimes the schools suffered. On December 25, 1861, just after the Southern Utah Mission arrived in St. George, the Santa Clara River flooded and washed away the Santa Clara schoolhouse.

Two days later, the Southern Utah Mission started to organize a school for 103 students in the day school and 48 students in the night school. Haden Church was the first teacher of both schools. As soon as the social hall was completed, work on four schoolhouses commenced, and all were in use by 1867. The town was divided geographically into four wards for church and school purposes.

By the turn of the 20th century, ward schools were so overcrowded that the courthouse and tabernacle were also used for classroom space. Due to the extreme need, one much-larger centralized school, the Woodward School, opened in 1901 and taught grades one through eight. St. George Stake Academy (the first iteration of Dixie State University) opened in 1911 and offered high school and college classes. In the mid-1930s, the St. George Elementary School (the "Annex") opened for the lower grades, and Woodward became a middle school. It was not until the early 1960s that the college and high school separated.

Each of the wards in St. George originally built its own one-room schoolhouse. Martha Cox taught students the names of states, capital cities, and lakes through song at the Third Ward School at the corner of 300 West and 300 North Streets. Edward H. Snow recalls attending the school under a Mr. Schultz in the late 1870s. One day, Snow and other students staged a battle using green gourds. The war moved from the playground into the schoolroom when class reconvened after lunch. Soon, the room was covered in gourd rinds. The teacher identified the guilty culprits and made them pick up every scrap. Each student had a 10-foot strip of the class to clean. When Snow outgrew the material taught in the one-room schoolhouse, he went on to Mr. Peck's school to learn mathematics on the top floor of the old St. George Hall on Main Street and St. George Boulevard. Later in life, he recalled, "If I learned anything at Peck's school, I cannot remember what it was."

Early school teachers taught students of all ages in one-room schoolhouses with limited books and supplies. McGuffey's readers were the most popular method of promoting students through grades. Previous generations did not have books with pictures like McGuffey's. When Utah became a state in 1896, schools became free as state schools. Until then, students paid about $2.50 a quarter, and school only lasted a few months.

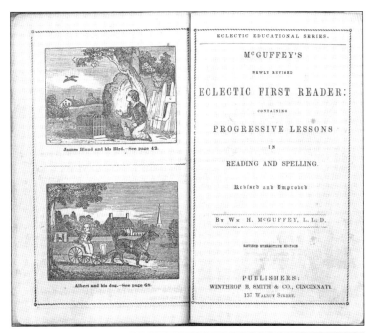

The Woodward School, built in 1899–1901, was a landmark in St. George education. For almost a hundred years, students attended school in the red sandstone building. Taken in the winter of 1936–1937, this photograph likely commemorated the unusual snowfall. Many longtime residents recall fun memories of their time inside its walls. Others, such as C.P. Snow, remember it as the "old red prison."

Becoming a sophomore at Woodward School was the highest education any student could get in St. George before 1913. The 1903 sophomore class had six girls and four boys, whose ages ranged from 22 to 17. In this picture of the first graduating class are, from left to right, Josephine Sandberg, James Cottam, Tillie Foster, Maud McFarlane Judd, Leo A. Snow, principal A.B. Christensen, Hattie Pike, Albertina "Bartie" Crosby, A.L. Larson, Josephine Snow Sandburg, and Angus M. Woodbury. Several students, like Snow and Woodbury, left St. George to pursue higher education. Snow came back to St. George to become the local engineer and surveyor. Woodbury went on to become a professor of zoology at the University of Utah in Salt Lake City and a naturalist at Zion National Park. The two Josephines later became sisters-in-law when Josephine Snow married Josephine Sandberg's brother.

As early as 1888, the town attempted to establish an academy. It was a short-lived enterprise that operated for five years out of the basement of the tabernacle. After the academy closed for the next 18 years, local students had to leave St. George to attend high school. The success of Woodward School in 1901 made another school building for upper grades necessary in order for students to continue their education locally. By 1909, the need for a high school spurred the St. George community to pay the majority of the costs to build the St. George Stake Academy on the corner of Main and 100 South Streets. Two years later, the school opened its doors to seven faculty members and 135 high school students. By 1916, it expanded to include teacher training and became a normal college and high school.

Two years after the St. George Stake Academy opened its doors, 13 students graduated. It was a momentous event and all the graduates gathered for a photograph, including John T. Woodbury Jr., LeRoy Hafen, George Seegmiller, Irvin Harmon, Dilworth Snow, Eldon Snow, N. Henry Savage, Florence Foremaster, principal Hugh M. Woodward, Annie Atkin, Gordon Riding, Persis Stratton, Karl Snow, Effie Frie, Walter Cottam, and Mattie Woodbury. High school graduates were still a rarity at this time in much of the United States, when less than 10 percent of the population finished high school. Some of the graduates went on to become professors, teachers, and naturalists. The graduates' parting words of advice were to wish the next students to continue striving "on and on and on" until they reached their goal.

The large letter "D" on the Black Hill first took shape in 1915 when Dixie Academy students used a lime and water mixture to whitewash rocks. An annual tradition was born when a new layer of paint was added each spring. Building the 100-by-75-foot "D" required an engineer, Leo A. Snow, to get it to look right.

The word "Dixie" in big white letters is painted on the Sugarloaf overlooking St. George. Many call the landmark the Dixie Rock. In 1914, the rock was painted by the seniors with "1914 D." Many think the "D" stood for Dixie, but it really stood for the Dolphin class. The high school students remain in charge of "Dixie," and the college students care for the "D" on the hill.

Late in 1916, the St. George Stake Academy added a second building to the campus, a gymnasium, just north of the original building on Main Street. The gymnasium was in use for almost 50 years by classes, faculty offices, cheerleaders, and the baseball and basketball teams. It was even the center for regular dances. Toward the end of the building's life, hometown fans were warned not to stomp on the second-floor bleachers, and teachers avoided school games for fear the building would collapse. The college asked the state legislature for a new gym in the early 1960s. The college received a new gym building (currently the Student Activity Center) on a new campus on the outskirts of town, which triggered the move of the campus from the old downtown campus to its new and current location.

Washington County Library 1918

Libraries and education were both highly valued in St. George. The first library association was incorporated in 1864, but it remained without a building. In 1910, the St. George Public Library and library board were established by Mayor George F. Whitehead, and Ida Miles was appointed the first librarian. In 1912, a Carnegie library grant application was submitted, and three years later, $8,000 was given to St. George for a new library. Income from taxes was used to purchase gymnasium equipment and books. The library building was erected in 1916 with the help of the community and Carnegie grants. The residents of St. George heavily used the library. The books were used so much that many of them had threadbare covers and worn pages. It was not until 1928 that a separate children's library was created in the basement.

In December 1924, the cast of *The Toreador*, an operetta by Woodward students, lined up for photographs between the Woodward School and Carnegie Library. Many teachers participated in making the play successful, including director Karl Larson; Earl Bleak, directing the orchestra; Annie Linder on piano; Bessie Thurston, choreography; and others managing costuming and stage design. In the old days, the audience would put molasses in barrels for admission, and the

barrels were traded in Salt Lake City for books that were used by the community. Woodward teachers were deeply engaged with their students, and they made do with far fewer resources than other Utah school districts, making the Carnegie Library a necessity. Teachers and students alike relied on the nearby library.

The science building was the third building added to the Dixie Normal College campus across the street from the gymnasium on Main Street. In 1927, the first floor was finished in time for the fall semester, and in the summer of 1928, a second floor was added. All of the science and mathematics courses were taught in the new building, which was equipped with new biology and chemistry labs and brand new equipment. The home economics department had a new modern kitchen and serving room where up-to-date cooking skills could be taught using appliances that students would regularly have in their homes as adults. The building also supported the agricultural sciences, which hosted a very successful poultry show and a canning center during the Great Depression. Through the years, the building was also a center of community life with lectures and adult evening classes.

The original Dixie College campus lined both sides of Main Street between Tabernacle and 100 South Streets. The LDS tabernacle and the academy were purposefully placed on the same block because the community wanted both to be in the heart of town and the center of community life. The college grew to encompass 11 buildings between 1911 and the early 1960s. The original academy building became known as the education building and was next door to the gymnasium. A recreation hall and library were added behind the gymnasium and tabernacle. Across Main Street from the education building were the LDS institute and Morris Dormitory for boys. Opposite the gymnasium was the Cannon Dormitory for girls and the industrial arts building. Facing the tabernacle was the science building. Of these buildings, only the original academy building and the tabernacle are still standing today.

If asked what their favorite school activity was, there is little doubt these happy children would say they loved their time on the playground. Recess has always been a time of activity and interest for children. In the 1932 school year, the students' favorite sports changed every few weeks. Some of the favorites worth mentioning were jumping ropes, practicing tosses with lasso ropes, and marbles in good weather.

The first 11 children from the Shivwits Reservation attended Woodward School with a Miss Madison as their teacher in 1932. Due to budget cuts that came with the Great Depression, teachers volunteered to teach two weeks without pay. Additionally, the school year was three weeks shorter than usual. Buildings did not get needed repairs, but most schools did get one new set of reference books for their libraries.

By the middle of the Great Depression, the Woodward School had more students than capacity. Planning for a new building started in 1933 with a request for federal New Deal funds. The new school, St. George Elementary (also known as the Annex), opened in 1936 for grades one through six, with 500 students enrolled, more than ever before. After the elementary school opened, the Woodward School building became a middle school for seventh and eighth grades. In 1936, the elementary school year started a week later than planned due to construction delays. Students had to go to class on two Saturdays to make up for the missed time. In 1937, a kindergarten class was offered for the first time in St. George in the new school. Students played many games common in today's parks. Other games, like this round of boxing, would no longer be permitted.

The Great Depression heavily impacted the college's finances. In 1933, the church relinquished control, and the community kept the college going for two years until Dixie Junior College became a state school. There were several years without a yearbook or student newspaper, but they still managed to celebrate. Lenore "Perk" Perkins was the 1938 athletic queen, a cheerleader leading college songs and yells, and was on a committee for amusements.

Falling snow is always a novelty in St. George. Even rarer are days with enough snow to make a good snowball. These Dixie Junior College students play in the snow between the college's education and gymnasium buildings in 1949. The recreation center is visible in the background. In the words of the students, "That ain't sunshine."

Many of the games and activities of the past would never meet today's safety standards. This game of tug-of-war in a muddy trench was a friendly competition between the college classes, and one lucky fellow was put in charge of digging the mud pit. The seniors sank in their tug against the juniors during their Boys' Day assembly event. The women watched the competition, cheering on the athletes, but did not participate in the sporting events. In contrast to the mens' muddy test of strength, the women were much more refined. Their Girls' Day assembly featured a variety of numbers as part of a fashion revue where tea was served. The day culminated in a very successful dance. The young women were even kind enough to publicly thank the female faculty members who helped sponsor the event.

In the late 1950s, Dixie College was still home to both the local high school and the junior college, which led some to view the college half as only a glorified high school. Debates among students began as some advocated separating the college from the high school. One student even publicly declared the greatest weakness of the college was being combined with the high school and being dragged down to their level. The first step students took was to distinguish between high school and college teams by designating separate mascots. The high school retained the traditional Flyers, while the college chose the Rebels as their mascot. Additionally, safety concerns about the stability of the original gymnasium necessitated a move to a new college campus in 1963, which effectively separated high school from college. The high school received a new campus in 1966.

High school football has been a staple in Utah since 1898. Dixie High School had 168 victories under coach Walter "Walt" Brooks, with 23 consecutive wins from 1973 to 1974. The team won the state championships in 1972–1974. Students and players always made sure to save a place for the coach's dad in the middle of the bleachers so he could attend all of the games and see the action.

As the head coach for 25 years, Walt Brooks attended all of the games and pep club rallies. His sister Willa Nita remembers her sons going to the rodeo and football games with their uncle Walt. Their favorite thing to do was collect pop bottles to exchange for hotdogs. Nothing was better than attending a game and eating a hotdog or two.

Silence was the number one rule at the Dixie College library. Fraternization was strictly prohibited, and too much talking could get students kicked out of the library and denied future privileges. Students were strongly requested to push in chairs and replace magazines in the correct position. It was the student's responsibility to return books directly to the librarian's hands. A 2¢ fine for being a day late returning a book could earn one a place on a bulletin board in the library that listed the students on the naughty list for all to see. One student cheekily suggested that talking was not the problem so much as the lack of an organization system for the magazines that caused disruptions in the library. The student was tired of looking for the most recent *Time* magazine only to find it under a stack of *Congressional Records*. But rules are rules, and she faithfully replaced the magazine back where she had found it.

Four

THE BUSINESS OF LIVING

The hand that's soiled by honest work
Is easy enough to clean;
But the hand that never touches dirt
Is sometimes deadly mean.
It matters not what a man may do
To make an honest living;
He's just as good as anyone else
If the best of himself he's giving.

—Mary Adeline Johnson Haws
1916

Hard work has been the hallmark of St. George and the surrounding towns. It is evident in the drastic growth of the city and the changes to the natural environment, although growth has not always been easy. In 1854, early Mormon missionaries found an old settlement of Tonaquint Native Americans farming wheat at the confluence of the Santa Clara and Virgin Rivers. Mormon pioneers sent to colonize St. George in 1861 brought along animals and seeds to develop a successful agriculture enterprise. They devoted incredible efforts to dam the Santa Clara and Virgin Rivers for irrigation. The grazing of local grasses eliminated a local Native American supply of nutritious seeds, and the dams cut off irrigation to Paiute fields. Paiute life was altered, and many went hungry in the following winters. As St. George grew, the Tonaquint population dwindled unnoticed by their white neighbors.

St. George residents also struggled to make a living their first few years combating hunger, a scarcity of drinking water, extreme elements, and disease. Despite all the difficulties, many stayed, made a living for themselves, and built a town with abundant social life, educational opportunities, and businesses. They made their livings through farming, cattle grazing, and bartering, as paper money was scarce for years. It was common for church members to pay their tithing in goods they had produced and to sell extra to the tithing office. In return, they would receive scrip that could be redeemed later. St. George was primarily agricultural, with initial ventures in producing cotton, silk, grapes, peaches, and sorghum molasses. A shift to traditional food crops helped the isolated community combat hunger, and it thrived. Over the years, turkeys, sugar beets, and ranching had their moments as essential crops. As the automobile became a household necessity, businesses shifted to focus on tourism.

Brigham Young originally called men to Southern Utah to convert local tribes, establish a southern trade route to California, and produce cotton. In 1858, nineteen-year-old Jacob Peart Jr. etched a cotton plant and the words, "I was se[n]t her[e] to rais[e] cotten," on the cliff overlooking the Virgin River. Today, both historical and new graffiti is visible near Interstate 15, exit 4.

By the 1900s, cotton was no longer grown in St. George on a large scale. With such an isolated and impoverished community, families could not thrive if they were barely surviving. They quickly realized that they had to reduce their cotton acreage and increase their sustenance farming with wheat, alfalfa, sugar beets, and other various vegetables. Although discouraged for personal use by local religious leaders, many also grew tobacco and grapes for wine.

Early St. George farmers combated the annual flooding of the Virgin and Santa Clara Rivers that swept away roads, dams, irrigation ditches, fields, shops, and homes. The town quickly realized the Santa Clara River was easier to control. It became the focus of farming and irrigation efforts in the 1860s. The Washington Fields Dam, pictured here, was completed in 1891 and tamed the Virgin River for almost a century.

Once the Washington Fields Dam and diversion canal were completed in the 1890s, more land downstream could be effectively farmed without fear that the Virgin River would swell and wash away crops. By 1903, the canal watered 1,660 acres planted with wheat, alfalfa, oats, and sorghum. The dam and canal were in use until a dike at Quail Creek Reservoir broke and washed out the canal.

Growing cotton in Southern Utah was different from growing it in the Southern states. Early cotton farmers learned, through trial and error, how to irrigate and work with the alkaline soil. Successfully growing cotton was still not enough to turn a profit. In 1868, Brigham Young personally invested in the cotton factory in Washington by the Virgin River to process the raw cotton and make it profitable in faraway markets.

Cotton prices plummeted at the end of the Civil War, and the transcontinental railroad made purchasing cotton less expensive than growing it in Southern Utah. The cotton factory started processing wool as well. The 1890s economic recession helped Thomas Judd make the mill profitable for a few years before it ceased production in 1898. Besides a short stint as a CCC camp, the building was neglected for almost 90 years.

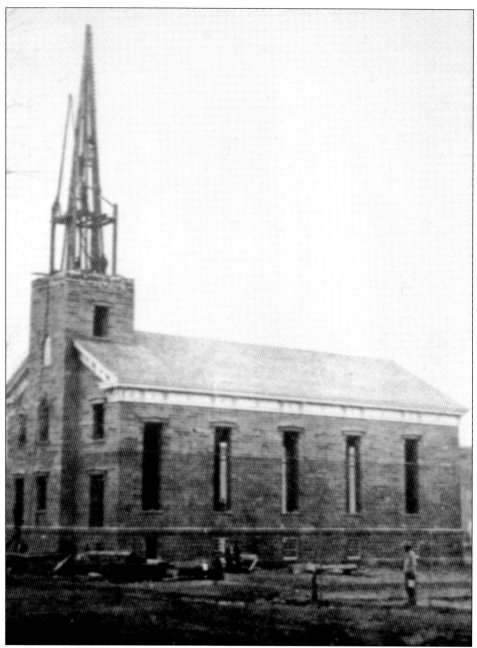

Construction on the St. George Tabernacle began within two years of the founding of St. George, and it was in use well before construction was completed 14 years later. Locals dedicated hard work quarrying the stone and building the large meeting hall. Tithing from Cedar City was diverted to help pay the expenses that building such a large structure incurred. The tabernacle was built to hold 2,000 people, much more than lived in the town for several decades. It was used for worship, classes, and cultural events. It even hosted several schools over the years until dedicated school buildings could be constructed. Locals set their watches to the clock at the top of the steeple. Water was measured by the minute and a shared common time reduced conflict over water use. The tabernacle continues to be a central gathering place in downtown St. George.

FIRST POST OFFICE BUILT IN STATE OF UTAH
IN 1863 BY JOHN PYMM - ST. GEORGE, UTAH
FRASHERS FOTO POMONA, CALIF.

In 1859, Toquerville established the first post office south of Cedar City. It was followed closely by Santa Clara and Washington City the same year. Before the St. George city survey was completed in 1862, Orson Pratt was named the first postmaster in St. George. That same year, residents petitioned for a mail route from Fillmore to Santa Clara and St. George, since the current route only came south to Cedar City. Before federal mail routes were established, locals created the Citizen's Mail, which was paid for by local taxes and served their immediate needs. The Citizen's Mail carried mail the last 60 miles from Cedar City to St. George. Even the state legislature hoped that the postmaster general would start a daily mail route between Salt Lake City and St. George. John Pymm became the second St. George postmaster in 1873, and built the first building used exclusively as a post office in St. George. The caption on this image claims it was the first post office in the state.

The St. George Co-Operative was founded in 1868 to help import merchandise such as glass, hardware, and tea that could not be produced locally. Church leaders like Erastus Snow and Robert Gardner were elected to the new board of directors, and locals initially invested $8,794. In the spring of 1869, freighters left St. George for San Francisco to pick up goods to start the store. On the trip, the horses went missing at the Mojave River, and the freighter Franklin Woolley was attacked and killed with arrows by Mojave Native Americans. The remaining men bought a casket and brought Woolley's body back to St. George for burial. A store was built on Main Street just north of the post office. Since money was scarce, it was common for a transaction to include bartering and the exchange of goods, so dividends were paid to the local stockholders in merchandise.

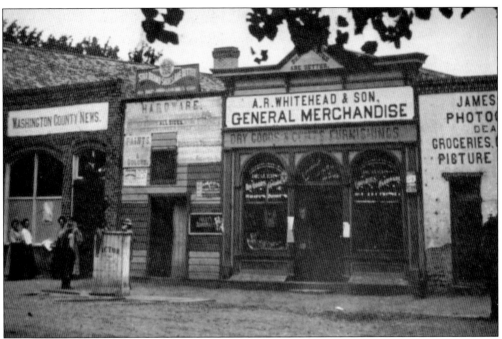

The first edition of the *Washington County News* rolled off the press in 1898 from its first location near Tabernacle and Main Streets. Among the advertisements was the newspaper's neighbor A.R. Whitehead & Son, dealers in general merchandise, who would also order furniture, carpets, and wallpaper on commission. Booth's Gallery, operated by photographer James J. Booth, also advertised with the promise of customer satisfaction guaranteed for photographs and enlargements.

ESSENCE OF LIFE.

For Pain in the Stomach or Bowels, Diarrhea, Dysentery, Colics, Wind in the Stomach, Cholera, Cholera Morbus, Cramps, Coughs, Neuralgia, Toothache, &c.

DIRECTIONS.—For troubles in the chest, an adult may take a teaspoonful, and children from three to twenty drops. every half hour, in a little water, until relieved. In other cases apply to affected part.

From J. E. JOHNSON,

ST. GEORGE AND SILVER REEF, - UTAH.

Other stores soon popped up in St. George, including drugstores. Johnson's Valley Tan Remedies was built on the corner of Main and Diagonal Streets. J.E. Johnson manufactured herbal medicinals that claimed to treat a colorful array of maladies, from "wind in the stomach" to a toothache, and could be ingested or topically applied. Some of these cure-all remedies were questionable.

For two short years in the early 1880s, Pickett, Riding, & Woodbury manufactured furniture and sold wallpaper, lumber, and shingles on 100 North Street near the post office. A few years later, Pickett partnered with E.B. Snow to provide an array of furniture and act as the local undertakers. In 1896, the partnership dissolved. Henry Riding continued carpentry work, and Snow opened a furniture store that lasted for decades.

IF NOT DELIVERED WITHIN TEN DAYS, RETURN TO

PICKETT, RIDING & WOODBURY.
BUILDERS,
DEALERS IN FURNITURE &C.
ST. GEORGE, UTAH.

Dodge's Spring was the local swimming hole where fun and relaxation were enjoyed by generations. In the late 1890s, the pond was filled with tasty watercress and fish. Dressing rooms were available for visitors. Through the early 1900s, it was a popular place for school trips, holidays, and picnics. A stick of dynamite was used one spring in an attempt to increase water flow. Instead, the pond drained.

There was no suitable land for the second generation of farmers to expand and build their own farms in Washington County. Residents dreamed big when they planned to bring water for irrigation to 2,000 acres of land on the Hurricane Bench to create more farmland. In 1893, the Hurricane Canal Company was formed to build a dam in the Virgin Narrows, a box canyon, and cut a seven-and-a-half-mile canal across a steep mountain that occasionally had to be tunneled. All the supplies were packed in, including anvils and other tools. All of the work was done by hand or with sticks of dynamite. It was slow going, with frequent landslides undoing days' worth of work in minutes. In 1904, water flowed through the newly completed canal, and Hurricane City was born. The Hurricane Canal is the story of common country folk who subdued the river and the mountain in defiance of the laws of nature and sound engineering principles.

In many ways, the mining town of Silver Reef was the opposite of St. George. Diverse people came together in search of silver rather than the Mormons, who sought isolation to practice their religion. More unmarried men lived in Silver Reef than in the rest of the county. The Catholic church and saloons were mainstays of the community. Despite the differences, the mining boom extended to St. George.

Geologists were surprised by Silver Reef because silver had never before been discovered in sandstone in the United States. Miners came from all over, especially from Pioche, Nevada. They began mining and processing the silver ore, with the height of the silver boon between the mid-1870s and the mid-1880s. Small efforts continued through the Great Depression until in the mid-1950s, when uranium was mined for a few years.

Many are surprised to hear that petroleum was an industry in St. George's early days. Significant markets for oil did not exist when exploratory wells found oil in 1907, since the automobile and gasoline industries did not yet exist. The first derrick to produce oil was Jack Martin's rig in Virgin near North Creek in January 1908. Several oil wells were drilled, but little was ever produced.

The first oil business, Virgin Dome Oil Company, in 1919, quickly sold out of stock at 10¢ a share. One of its advertisements summed up the oil industry: "If oil is struck we all win. If it fails we all lose. We hope we win." Ten years later, the company had drilled almost 3,000 feet without successful production in the Purgatory Flat area between Washington City and Hurricane City.

Five years after drilling started at the Virgin Oil Dome, drilling for oil took on new life when federal lands opened to prospectors. A few years later, in 1926, approximately 15 men formed the Washington County Oil Development Company to test petroleum reserve No. 7 for oil in the newly opened land. Another oil prospect was already drilling the Bloomington Dome reserve No. 1.

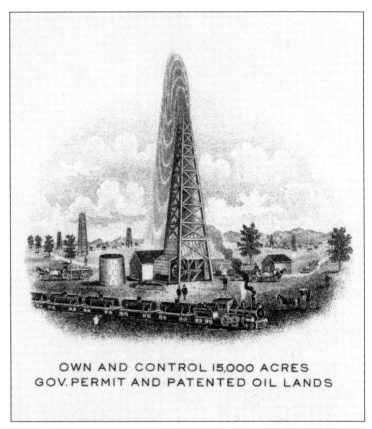

OWN AND CONTROL 15,000 ACRES
GOV. PERMIT AND PATENTED OIL LANDS

Oil extraction in Southwest Utah was in its heyday in the 1920s through the mid-1930s after the automobile brought global demand for petroleum. The early oil fields were in Virgin, and later, several wells started in St. George. In March 1935, there was an accident at a St. George oil rig that killed 10 people and blew up the well, ending the excitement over oil production.

Cattle ranching was not for the faint of heart. Ranchers and their cattle hands could be gone for weeks at a time. Between summer and winter, they searched the Arizona Strip and Southern Utah for missing cows as they drove herds to greener pastures. When they returned home after days of back-breaking labor, the ranchers wanted a place away from the women where they could drink and tell stories. As said by Rowland Rider, this is how the Roll Away Saloon was born. The women in Fredonia and Kanab did not like their husbands coming home past dinner and so intoxicated that they could not unsaddle their horses. They organized a posse to burn the place down. The men feared their women, so they built a small saloon on wood rollers that could be pushed either direction over the state line between Utah and Arizona. The strategy was enough to deter the wives from burning down the saloon because it was in another state. This conflict went on for years and kept the men's favorite drinking spot safe from their wives.

Over time, it became evident that ranching was better suited to the harsh environment than farming. In the early days, a herder was appointed to care for the milk cows and stock during the night. Every morning, it was his job to gather everyone's stock to be let out for the day and keep an eye on them grazing, so Native Americans did not drive them off.

Cowboys lived for weeks under the open sky during the cattle drive as they rounded up cattle for market and drove them through the range. To survive, a chuckwagon hauled necessary supplies and provided each cowhand three meals a day. This wagon was most likely covered with a repurposed wagon cover from the US military.

The *Washington County News* stopped production for eight years and returned in 1908 in a new facility near the corner of St. George Boulevard and Main Street. Along the boulevard was a two-story post office operated by Samuel Judd. At a time when most businesses were closed on Sundays, the post office was open for one hour on Sundays and even holidays.

When the *Washington County News* started publishing again in 1908, it reduced the cost to $1.50 for pre-paid annual subscriptions. To increase circulation, the paper charged 50¢ less than its price in 1900 before it was discontinued. The newspaper also had the newest styles of type and larger production equipment. The paper's editor promised it was there to stay this time, and it continued publication for another 80 years.

In 1930, the population of St. George was still under 2,500, and the size of the town reflected its people. Back then, the LDS temple was on the outskirts of town with only open fields between it and the Virgin River to the south, Black Hill to the west, and the east ridge. Prior to the construction of Sunbowl Stadium, the Dixie Round-Up Rodeo was held at the racetrack in the undeveloped area to the north of the temple. Spectators enjoyed both horse racing and rodeo in the same location. Once the Sunbowl was completed as the new home of the rodeo, competitors and crowds did not have as far to travel. To the north and northwest of the temple, most of the original homes were built close to water sources, but much has changed since the 1930s. The population has swelled to over 165,000, and Washington County is now the largest metro consumer of water per capita in the Southwest United States.

By the Great Depression, several canals and dams were in full operation, controlling flooding of the Virgin and Santa Clara Rivers. Floods still regularly occurred, but they rarely washed out the dams, canals, and bridges. Several steel and concrete bridges were built across the Virgin River in the first two decades of the 20th century. The Virgin River Bridge was the main connecting point in St. George for 65 years. By 1985, the bridge was no longer in use and was washed away in 1988 when the Quail Creek dike failed. Over the years, there were a few close calls when the water rose almost to the floor beams or washed away the support piles.

In the 1930s, the US Department of Agriculture began experimenting with growing a disease-resistant variety of sugar beets for seed production in St. George. Soon after, the Utah and Idaho Sugar Company introduced a beet seed plant in the old opera house. Beet seeds were cleaned, tested for moisture and germination, and then packaged for sale throughout the Intermountain West. Sugar beets were processed into refined white sugar.

The weather of St. George is ideal for growing sugar beets for seed since it stays warm enough for the beets to winter in the fields and be harvested in the fall. Sugar beet seeds were harvested with a self-propelled pick-up thrasher. In 1934, the crop of sugar beet seeds was estimated to weigh around 450 tons and was worth around $80,000.

Local business on Main Street in St. George in the 1930s and 1940s included well-remembered restaurants and soda fountains like the Big Hand Cafe (101 North Street) and Whiteway's Ice Cream and Malt Shop (99 North Street). Main Street also boasted a Poultrymen's Hatchery, where local farmers and hobbyists could purchase baby chicks and turkey poults. The store carried a variety known as "Dixie doubles," known for being double tested and double the profit.

On Main Street just south of the Big Hand Cafe and Whiteway's were Dixie Jewelry (79 North Street) and the California Inn (75 North Street), both of which were in business through the late 1930s to the late 1960s. More than rings and watches were sold at Dixie Jewelry, which also offered silverware, pens, and dresser sets. The California Inn sold cigars, pipes, stuffed toys, and Western novelties.

Across the nation, the New Deal funded public works projects during the Great Depression. The CCC camp in St. George built the Winsor (Shem) Dam on the Santa Clara River in 1934 to help with flood control. Originally, the dam was called the Winsor Dam, named for the engineer who designed it, Luther Winsor. Leo A. Snow was the CCC engineer assigned to build the dam.

The Winsor (Shem) Dam replaced an earlier dam of brush covered with sand that was frequently damaged by flooding. The new dam was a vast improvement at over 750 feet along the top. In 1938 and 1955, heavy rains damaged parts of the spillway, and each time the dam was fixed because farmers in Santa Clara and St. George relied on the diversion of water for irrigation.

Several changes came to St. George as a result of the New Deal during the Great Depression. Houses and streets were numbered, and new street signs were added to help locals give visitors directions without using their hands and feet. The new addresses must have been a great help to the postmaster, as the new post office was built in 1937 on Tabernacle and First East Streets. It had 566 post office boxes to allow for future growth. A newspaper article announcing the new post office had to explain why the boxes were locked and that the keys were merely borrowed. The postmaster, Will Brooks, had a new office with every convenience, with the minor exception that the government did not include cooling systems in new buildings. Other federal agencies, such as the forestry department, used the basement for office space over the years. By 1985, the post office was outgrown, and a new one was built the same year.

In 1945, turkey production was hailed as the outstanding industry in Washington County after growing rapidly in just a few years. The isolation of St. George was actually a positive in turkey production since it meant flocks and farms could be isolated, preventing the spread of disease among the birds. Farmers throughout the state wanted to buy locally since many poults arrived ill after long-distance shipping. Turkey farming remained very successful for two decades, with hatcheries, farms, and production plants in towns throughout the county. One employee of a turkey processing plant recalls his job was to catch the turkeys before they were dispatched and cleaned. He then cleaned up the feathers, taking truckloads down to the Virgin River and dumping them. He joked that the water took the feathers downstream to Lake Mead, where they must have become part of Las Vegas's drinking water.

The first annual Dixie Round-Up Rodeo, sponsored by the Lion's Club, was held in 1935. In 1947, it was held in the historic Sunbowl Stadium for the first time. For 40 years, it was one of the few rodeo grounds where cowboys competed on grass. The rodeo was initially held on land southwest of the Sunbowl in the middle of a racetrack. The unique design of the Sunbowl and its location on the edge of downtown made it an ideal venue for the rodeo. It still stands today on the corner of 100 South and 400 East Streets.

The Round-Up parade and rodeo was the main September event in St. George that no one in the county wanted to miss. In addition to a rodeo queen competition, activities included bull riding, mutton busting, barrel racing, and roping. The rodeo has survived because of the continued support of the Lions Club and the community. This shy cow is not falling for the temptation of hay offered by Maurine Whipple.

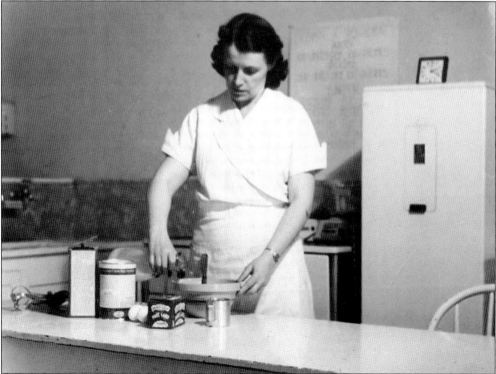

Traditional women's work changed drastically in the first half of the 20th century with the introduction of electricity and appliances. Advances such as research on vitamins added a scientific approach to housework. Electric stoves helped remove a lot of uncertainty and perhaps even drudgery from cooking. Home economics classes taught practical applications of these new tools and efficiency of home management.

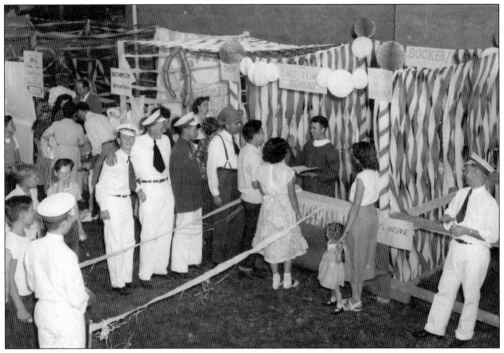

The Building a Better Community contest in 1950 spurred a St. George women's club into action. It took home the prize for its three-stage approach. The club created an exhibit of cultural arts, put on a college carnival complete with a marriage booth to raise funds for a new women's dormitory, and held a community beautification project. Women worked together to make St. George a better community.

Social activities sponsored by women's clubs were critical in the development of the community. Some events were organized donation drives, while others were educational or social events. Regardless of the type of event, women used their homemaking skills to further their cause, even if that meant baking 300 pies for a bake sale.

Locals entirely funded the first efforts to produce oil. As the wells were drilled deeper, with little to show for the work, experts from California were called in to help fund and manage the expensive operations. Most of the oil-mining industry faded in the 1930s, but there were still operations southeast of St. George at the Escalante oil dome in the early 1950s.

The Dixie Pioneer Memorial Hospital was built in 1952 to replace the McGregor Hospital. When the hospital opened, a night's stay cost $8–10, about the same as a hotel room, but the visit came with meals. The building was judged too small to continue operations, with only 30 beds. It was torn down in 1975 and replaced by the larger Dixie Regional Medical Center.

As ranching evolved, so did the tools used to manage herds of cattle. The cattle chute or "squeeze" was used for sorting, moving, and treating cows and is now standard equipment on ranches. Instead of having to rope each animal one at a time, ranchers used the "squeeze" for pregnancy checks, branding, tagging, and as pictured here, castrating young males destined for the market.

The large-scale turkey industry may have failed in the early 1960s, but poultry continued to have a presence in St. George. Small incubators used at home and with youth groups like the 4-H Club and Future Farmers of America maintained the legacy of raising chicks and poults. Large units hold up to 400 eggs for the 21–28 day incubation period and keep production local on a small scale.

Bill Barlocker owned the most successful and largest turkey farm in Washington County. In 1959, his farm produced over 300,000 poults and three million pounds of turkey meat and sold turkey eggs in 33 states as one of the largest turkey producers in the world. At the height of his success, he served as a three-term mayor of St. George and came within 20,000 votes of being elected governor. His success came to an end with the assassination of Pres. John F. Kennedy in November 1963. Many Americans fasted as a way to mourn for their lost president, causing turkey sales for Thanksgiving to plummet. Barlocker could not sell the 350,000 frozen turkeys he had on hand and lost everything but some land. The local industry never recovered. In 1965, Barlocker was on the slopes of Cedar Mountain, herding sheep for a living.

Before the Taylor Grazing Act of 1934, public land was freely used by cattlemen and sheep ranchers for water and grazing. At the height of sheep ranching, one herding outfit had almost 40,000 sheep. A resident recalled when his grandfather and father found 1,200 head of sheep on their range. When they caught up with the sheepherder, he did not even know he had lost them.

Herds of sheep were maintained for wool. Sheep were difficult to raise because of the constant care needed to protect them from becoming prey to wild animals. Pregnant sheep gave birth in the spring, followed by wool shearing. Some wool would be set aside for local use, but the majority was shipped north to Salt Lake City to be sold to woolen mills.

Between 1951 and 1963, a total of 100 aboveground nuclear tests were conducted at the Nevada Test Site. In 1953, radiation killed thousands of sheep in Southern Utah. Some were severely burned, and radiation caused miscarriages and deformities in newborn lambs. Smaller sheep ranchers lost everything, while larger operations lost about one-third of their herds. By the late 1950s, cancer clusters grew, and those exposed became known as downwinders.

Southwest Utah relies on dams and pipelines to deliver essential water to fields, farms, and homes. When summer temperatures routinely hit over 105 degrees, the reservoirs created by the dams provided excellent recreational opportunities for fishing, swimming, boating, and other fun-filled activities. The Baker Reservoir was built in the early 1950s and is known for its rainbow and brown trout.

Peaches have been a cornerstone crop grown locally since St. George was settled. Peaches grew on 64 acres in Washington County. In 1862, the tithing office set the price of dried peaches at 30¢ per pound. Peaches were even distilled into liquor at one point. In 1908, St. George held a fruit day to demonstrate that the Elberta peach was viable for commercial markets. Peaches have held steady ever since.

Peaches from Washington County hit national markets starting in the 1930s, with truckloads heading to states as far away as Montana and Texas. The introduction of the Elberta peach made peaches more marketable. Local farmers still had to combat infections, mildew, fluctuations in weather, and national prices to make a living. The orchards have become smaller over the years as production has decreased.

St. George has a long history of growing and preserving a variety of fruits and vegetables. In 1868, an estimated 2,000–3,000 cans of fruit were put up. Women in both world wars were asked to can homegrown produce to help with national shortages. A cannery was set up during the Great Depression in St. George to help preserve local foods. For many, the habit continued.

Well into the 20th century, St. George was a city in isolation. Looking at the town of St. George from a distance with its white temple and "D" on the hill must have been a welcome sight for travelers coming through the desert. While either too much or not enough water has always been a concern in St. George, the Virgin River is what drew settlers to the area.

The Glen Canyon Dam was completed in 1963, and as it was filling, the newly created Lake Powell was already hosting tours. It is the second-largest human-made lake in the United States. At left, a small portion of Navajo Mountain is visible. While the lake is a three-hour drive away, it has been an economic boon for tourism in St. George.

For three days in early December 1966, it rained heavily, setting records for the highest one-day rainfall in multiple towns upstream. Runoff caused the Virgin River to swell to its highest level since St. George was founded in 1861. The river was approximately 60 percent higher than during the last big flood in the 1930s, and it damaged a portion of the River Road Bridge.

St. George is in the midst of a vast desert where annual rainfall is only around 10 inches each year. Anytime it rains more than an inch per day, there is a chance of a flash flood as water streams down previously dry creek beds, which then pour into the Virgin River. In 1984, a flash flood built enough momentum to push a wall of debris.

Rainfall in the center of St. George can occasionally result in water flowing through the streets from Red Hill and Black Hill south toward the river. Many of the roads have been designed to accommodate runoff. Flood Street, for example, has a distinct "V" shape to direct water away from homes. While helpful, it can make driving a bit more tricky.

Just before midnight on December 31, 1988, families living downstream from the Quail Creek Reservoir were jolted awake. The dike was failing, and everyone in its path needed to be evacuated from their homes. At 1,980 feet long and 78 feet tall, the dike was struggling against the overwhelming pressure of the water. For 30 heart-stopping minutes, everyone waited in hopes that it would stand strong. Unfortunately, the erosion continued until just after midnight on January 1, 1989, when the dam was breached, releasing 25,000 acre-feet of water onto everything downstream. Water rushed through a 300-foot-by-90-foot break in the dike, washing out the old Virgin River Bridge, roads, crops, equipment, and livestock. The damage was extensive, including the Washington Fields Dam, 30 homes, and 58 apartments. The Washington Fields Dam was rebuilt the following year.

Five

Transformation from a Small Town

St. George was not the first town settled in Washington County, but it was intended as a larger and more stable community. As the new town successfully built social, educational, and religious institutions, it encouraged growth and became a hub for the smaller outlying Mormon colonies.

The first tourism started in 1877, with faithful saints traveling to the first temple completed in the West. Newly engaged couples traveling with chaperones or newlyweds would travel from Arizona along the aptly named Honeymoon Trail.

With the introduction of the automobile, new roads offered new opportunities. Avid motorists sought the best route between Los Angeles and Salt Lake City through a barren desert where roads did not yet exist. Due in large part to strong advocates like Charles Biglow, St. George found itself right in the middle of the route.

The landscape around St. George is rugged, and the railroad was never extended south past Cedar City. The landscape again played a role when the Interstate Highway System was introduced in the 1950s, although it took an additional 20 years for Interstate 15 to be completed through St. George. The incomplete section of I-15 required a detour through Santa Clara and over Utah Hill until the treacherous portion through the Virgin River Gorge was completed.

Restaurants and motels popped up all across St. George as tourism became an integral portion of the economy. Over time, St. George has been publicized for its easy access to national and state parks, its 300 days of sun a year, and even its golf courses. It is a favorite place for many "snowbirds" to spend the winter. LDS president Brigham Young was the first in 1870 to begin spending his winters in St. George. The story of St. George would be incomplete without the mention of its visitors.

From his winter home in Southern Utah, Brigham Young asked the people of St. George if they would build a temple. With a resounding "yes," work was quickly started. Over the next six years, men, women, and even children helped contribute to every step of construction. The volcanic rock for the fountain was procured from Black Hill, while the sandstone was quarried from Red Hill and lumber came from Pine Valley or Mount Trumbull in the Arizona Strip. The St. George Temple was not completed until 1877, and for many years, it was the only operating LDS temple. Bridal parties traveled from near and far. Many of the faithful traveled for weeks along the Honeymoon Trail from settlements in Northern Arizona to be married and sealed in the temple. The temple continues to be a cornerstone of the community and has had two major renovations over the years.

OX TEAM THAT HALLED THE FONT TO ST. GEORGE TEMPLE ABOUT 1874. FROM SALT LAKE CITY.

In 1871, Brigham Young called for a temple to be built in St. George. Six years of labor culminated in one of the most significant accomplishments of St. George's early residents. As a young man in 1873, C.L. Christensen remembers working on the construction of the temple. Two years later, in July 1875, Christensen was part of a team that helped pick up the cast iron baptismal font from the Southern Utah Railroad's southernmost point in Juab County. Of the three teams of young men, Christensen recalled using three yokes of oxen to haul the 2,900-pound load back to St. George in 119-degree weather. The St. George temple was the only Western temple built without the benefit of railroads and shipped-in supplies. Freighters like Christensen picked up the glass for the windows in California. The temple was dedicated on April 6, 1877, and remains the oldest functioning LDS temple.

John D. Lee & Family

The Honeymoon Trail, also called the Mormon Wagon Road, was vital in connecting the remote ranches and settlements of Little Colorado and the Arizona Strip to the larger town of St. George. The Grand Canyon, formed by the Colorado River, divides much of Arizona and Utah. Lee's Ferry is the only place to cross the river for hundreds of miles. From Lee's Ferry, the Honeymoon Trail continues through Houserock Valley to Pipe Springs, and then into St. George. The river crossing at Lee's Ferry had been a favorite of Native Americans before being used by the Dominguez-Escalante Expedition in 1776. Nearly a century after the first recorded white use of the ferry, John D. Lee and his family set up the first permanent ferry service while hiding from the law. Although Lee himself only operated the site for four years, and his family for less than a decade, the location has retained his name.

In 1896, Lee's Ferry was transferred to Jim Emmet. Concerned about the number of boats lost downriver during high water, Emmet built a cable system in 1899 to move people across the river. The new ferry location was upstream and part of Emmet's bigger plan of making a living. He built a new dugway over Lee's Backbone to make it safer and wanted to charge a toll.

Water is a rare commodity in the desert. Pipe Springs provided essential water for the Kaibab band of Paiutes before Mormon ranchers erected a two-building fort with an enclosed courtyard over the spring. It became a stopping point for travelers along the Honeymoon Trail. In the 1920s, Pipe Springs, halfway between Zion and Grand Canyon National Parks, became a national monument and was frequently visited by tourists.

Lumber was hauled from Mount Trumbull in Arizona to aid the construction of the St. George Temple. The lumber route became known as the Honeymoon Trail and was a heavily traveled road between Mormon colonies in Arizona and St. George. The route continued to be important to the ranchers of the Arizona Strip, and reenactments of the trail were part of a pageant coinciding with the Dixie Round-Up Rodeo.

In 1881, four years after the St. George Temple was finished, the first group of Mormon pioneers traveled over 400 miles for about six weeks through the barren desert to be married in the temple. Water and forage food for the teams pulling the wagons were hard to come by on the route. Many who made the arduous journey spent several weeks in St. George visiting family and friends.

Brigham Young chose the location of the St. George Temple, and it remained on the outskirts of town for several decades. Now in the heart of the city, it is visible for miles. At the turn of the 20th century, there was no professional landscaping, just a beautiful, brilliant white building rising from the desert. The temple grounds are now an oasis in the desert filled with palm trees and lawns.

Little is said of the men and women who have served at the temple beyond the presidencies. However, the work they complete could not be carried out without the help of the ordinary women, some of whom are perhaps seen here arriving on the temple wagon. The temple sits six blocks from downtown St. George and is still one of the most visited places in Washington County.

The Sugarloaf is quite possibly St. George's most popular and earliest recreation area. It gained its name from its resemblance to the solid chunks of sugar sold when pioneers first settled the area. It is a playground for picnics, climbers, and hikers. In 1872, John W. Young deeded the Sugarloaf to the City of St. George, and it has remained a centerpiece of the city's park system.

On a trip to an oil outcrop in 1908, Leo A. Snow saddled up his horse for the journey. Horses played a vital role in transportation. In 1902, few city ordinances regulated riding or driving within city limits. They did require four-foot hitching posts in front of businesses and for unsupervised animals to be tied up. Riding on sidewalks and servicing stallions in public was prohibited.

By 1912, the Southern Utah Telephone Company had already established a one-line connection to Salt Lake City. Telephone lines edged the heavily used and unpaved intersection at Tabernacle and 100 West Streets. People from outlying towns were often a day's ride from the nearest phone until the Peoples Progressive Telephone Company was formed by Washington County men with the dream of bringing telephones to the remote towns and ranches.

Henry Ford's assembly line revolutionized the automobile industry in 1913. A year later, St. George began hosting Good Roads Days to develop its roads. On one Good Roads Day in 1917, people from ages 14 to 80 volunteered, with almost the entire college present, and businesses were asked to shut down and give employees a working holiday. Relief societies from both towns prepared lunches for all the workers.

A Dodge touring car parked next to a horse hitched to a post in front of the original courthouse demonstrates the overlapping of new and old technologies on St. George Boulevard, when it was still a dirt road. In 1915, St. George still required hitching posts in front of public buildings with rules regulating how horses should be handled. For the first time, the town developed ordinances for "self-propelled," "riding machines," and "horseless carriages." The new safety rules included requiring brakes, lights, and a horn on every automobile to sound when approaching other vehicles. Speed limits were set to "reasonable and proper" with the driver in "immediate control" of the car in a way that does not "endanger life and limb." There were even new environmental controls, such as prohibiting idling a vehicle for more than 10 minutes and not allowing for visible exhaust.

Mukuntuweap was first established as a national monument in 1909. When the first accessible road was built in 1917, the monument was expanded, and the name changed to Zion National Park. Advocates of the Arrowhead Trail promoted St. George's proximity to Zion as an attraction worth visiting. Over the years, many locals have enjoyed day trips to the park. The local Dixie College even had annual trips there in the late 1930s for group hikes, games, and campfire programs. In 1936, about 124,000 people visited Zion National Park each year, compared to approximately 4.3 million people annually today. Tourism to the park, most of which is within Washington County's borders, brings tourists from across the globe to see the beautiful sights.

In 1916, a small six-room hotel at the corner of Main and Tabernacle Streets changed ownership and became the Arrowhead Hotel. It was named after the Arrowhead Trail, which connected St. George to the broader world and opened the possibility of a tourism-based economy. By 1933, the hotel had increased its capacity to 50 rooms. It was known as an excellent hotel with a home-like and restful atmosphere.

Developing the roads between Los Angeles and Salt Lake City was an expensive and collaborative process. The Arrowhead Trail Improvement and Development Association had participation from small towns like St. George, Beaver, Parowan, Fillmore, Delta, and Rockville in Utah, as well as Las Vegas and Kingman, Arizona. Small towns developed their roads to ensure the boon to their economies and their place on the main travel route.

On the Good Roads Day in February 1917, a total of 347 men from St. George and Santa Clara volunteered with 92 plows and road scrapers to fix one of the worst stretches of the new automobile route between Los Angeles and Salt Lake City. The Arrowhead Trail Association was instrumental in organizing the event and believed highway improvement made for the successful development of remote communities.

From its start, St. George struggled to build a strong economy. Farming was incredibly tricky with little water. The advent of the automobile brought new possibilities. Charles Bigelow and members of the Arrowhead Trail began marketing St. George and the surrounding areas as places tourists could finally access. Roads were improved, St. George earned a spot on a major route, and new service industries quickly appeared.

Automobiles changed American life as new vehicles hit the roads, and garages, gas stations, and hotels met the new demand. Alma James Johnstun operated Jim's Garage between 1924 and 1932, where he sold Goodyear and Goodrich tires and cars like the $1,125 Willys-Knight. Next door was the St. George Hotel. In 1928, the hotel was renovated, adding a third floor and increasing the number of rooms to 35.

In the 1920s, St. George had two camps advertising plenty of shade for automobile tourists to choose from. Eventually, cabins were added, and visitors could pull their car up to their cabin door. Gas stations were added to some camps to increase profits. Cabins included a bed and a bathroom, and some boasted kitchenettes. Eventually, swamp coolers were added to allow visitors a comfortable stay, even in the summer.

In 1924, *Deadwood Coach* was the first full-length movie filmed in Zion National Park, which was portrayed as the Dakota Badlands. Tom Mix starred as Jimmie Gordon the Orphan with Tony the Wonderhorse. Over the years, Southern Utah has become a favorite filming location among studios with its varying landscape and breathtaking cliffs. St. George is home to films like *High School Musical* and *Butch Cassidy and the Sundance Kid*.

One of the main attractions in Zion National Park is the world-renowned hike of Angels Landing, which was cut into the rock in 1926. It dares visitors with a strenuous climb up a series of switchbacks followed by another climb across a long and narrow cliff with an almost 5,800-foot drop. The trail ends in a nearly 360-degree view of the surrounding canyon and Virgin River.

A much-more accessible view within Zion National Park is found at the Emerald Pools, just a short hike from the Zion Lodge. The upper and lower pools are calm and offer a cool place to relax on a hot day. The pools are fed by drainage from the cliffs above and by the "weeping" as water filters down through the rocks and collects in the pools.

A thousand people attended the opening of Hotel Liberty in 1928 at 100 East Street and St. George Boulevard. Two years later, a three-story addition almost doubled capacity, offering 65 rooms. A Liberty Cafe and Drugstore also provided for guests' needs in keeping with the slogan, "strangers register here as guests and not as a number." Hotel employees were known for their friendly and attentive service.

The Mount Carmel Tunnel in Zion National Park was completed in 1930 after almost three years of construction, which cost just over a half-million dollars. Construction started by lowering men on ropes or scaling ladders to bore the gallery openings into the face of the mountain, which were then connected to form the 1.1-mile tunnel. This national historic place remains a popular tourist destination.

The Big Hand Cafe opened in the early 1930s on the corner of Main Street and St. George Boulevard. A large neon hand pointed to the entrance and gave the cafe its name. Tourism was already a significant part of the economy, and the Greyhound bus stopped right in front of the Big Hand. The cafe was among the first buildings in St. George to tempt travelers with air conditioning.

Along with new businesses catering to drivers came billboards and posters advertising auto-related products. A horseless carriage was used years later to promote Texaco's Fire-Chief gasoline introduced in 1932, which was known for reducing engine knocking, surpassing government regulations, and having higher octane. Billboards in the background recommend Standard Red Crown Gasoline, "a new superfuel," and Conoco gasoline. St. George's position on the main route encouraged the growth of a service industry.

When the US Highway system was numbered in 1926, the Arrowhead Trail became known as Highway 91. After the interstate highway system started in the 1950s, the highway traveled through Santa Clara, St. George, Washington, and Leeds before connecting back to Interstate 15. Being on the main road was a boost to the smaller towns. Service and gas stations met customer needs and brought much-needed money into the county.

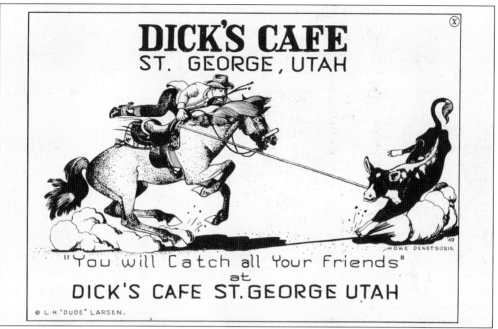

Dick's Cafe opened in 1935 as a small hamburger stand with eight stools on the corner of 100 East Street and St. George Boulevard and quickly became one of the busiest restaurants in town. In 1939, it was expanded with a new counter, front room, and neon signs for a modern appearance. The original owner was a rodeo contestant and supporter of the local Dixie Round-Up. The cafe was demolished in 1999.

In 1940, the Milne Motor Court was built at 300 East Street and St. George Boulevard, next to the Milne Sinclair service station. The motor court catered to auto travelers, with a private garage attached to each unit. It also offered all the modern amenities such as air conditioning and steam heating in all the cottages. Private baths, carpeted rooms, and Beautyrest mattresses provided comfort on the road.

Sugar Loaf Cafe – St. George, Utah

The Sugar Loaf Cafe opened in 1946 with an entire meal that cost only 50¢ and included everything from soup to dessert. Later, the cafe was moved to the corner of 300 East Street and St. George Boulevard, where it was one of the three large restaurants in town. The economy of St. George was reliant on tourism along Highway 91, and on and agriculture.

UFO sightings were frequent from the late 1940s to the 1970s, mainly due to the Roswell incident in 1947. Sometimes natural occurrences in the atmosphere are responsible rather than aliens. Lenticular clouds, commonly called UFO clouds because of their striking resemblance to UFOs, are formed over mountains or landmasses where the air is drawn upward.

118

Over time, there was a gradual shift away from the hotel layout to the motel design to meet customer preferences. In the early 1950s, near the corner of 200 East Street and St. George Boulevard, Hail's Motel offered tiled baths, carpets, air conditioning, and radios in each room. Today, the motel is still operating under the name Dixie Palm Motel.

The Sands Motel opened in 1953 on St. George Boulevard. It was one of the only motels with a second story in town and boasted the largest pool in the area. It even had a shallow end for children, drawing many tourists with families. Many of the roadside motels did not survive, but the Sands remains, with a retro look and small-town feel that charms visitors.

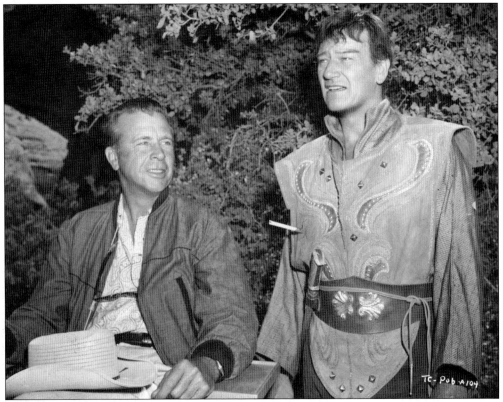

The Conqueror was filmed in Snow Canyon State Park in 1954. Just one year before, the US military conducted 11 aboveground nuclear tests in Yucca Flats. The wind carried the fallout to St. George and Snow Canyon, contaminating residents. Authorities reported the area safe, but it was discovered that the purpose of the tests was to see how radiation affected living things. Residents were only compensated after decades of court battles. Out of the 220 cast and crew members for *The Conqueror*, John Wayne, Susan Hayward, and 90 others died of cancer. There is no official record of the hundreds of Native American extras, so the actual number is probably higher.

The Conqueror was a flop at the box office in 1956, and many felt that the lead role was miscast and not a good fit for John Wayne. Although the movie was not successful, it showcased what a fantastic range of scenery St. George had to offer the movie industry. Southern Utah became a popular filming location for Westerns and science-fiction movies, which helped the local economy.

Before designation as a state park in 1958, Snow Canyon was a local favorite place to hike and picnic for decades. As early as 1928, locals advocated for a road through the canyon. It remained accessible only by horse until 1941, when a road was constructed. Locals wanted Snow Canyon on the tourist route, but it was the possibility of filming movies there that garnered state support for the road.

They Came to Cordura, starring Gary Cooper and Rita Hayworth, was filmed in 1958 in St. George and the surrounding areas. The story follows the 1916 Punitive Expedition to find Pancho Villa. The cast and crew traveled like a small mobile town, with numerous trailers, generators for electricity, and tanks of water to keep everyone hydrated in the hot desert sun.

Above the rim of Snow Canyon are two cinder cone volcanoes in the Diamond Valley area collectively called the Santa Clara Volcano. While the volcanoes are now extinct, the lava fields are evident in the black igneous rock formations in St. George and Santa Clara. In Snow Canyon, extinct lava flow tubes offer spelunkers caves to explore. The cones provide hikers a high vantage point with a great view.

In the northwest corner of Arizona is the Virgin River Gorge, a 500 million-year-old canyon carved by the Virgin River. In the late 1820s, Jedidiah Smith was the first white man to record his travels through the gorge. The following year, he sought an alternate route that led him over Utah Hill. In many ways, Smith's trips echo the later development of national roads.

Until the section of Interstate 15 through the gorge was completed in 1973, the freeway diverted to US Highway 91 through Santa Clara and over Utah Hill, which was still not a comfortable trip. The hill is steep and the area hot, which led to many radiators overheating. Local children took advantage of the steaming cars to sell water to those in need.

The Virgin River Gorge runs through Arizona and connects Utah to Nevada. It is a vital part of Utah's economy, which led the state to help fund that section of the interstate. The construction of I-15 through the gorge was the most expensive section of rural highway built at the time, at $100 per inch. The river was rerouted 12 times, necessitating five bridges. Flash flooding and quicksand caused problems during construction.

The completion of Interstate 15 transformed the small isolated town of St. George into a common stopover for all kinds of vehicles, especially semi-trucks. The 18-wheeler pictured here boasts an images of the show *Dukes of Hazzard*, popular in the 1970s and 1980s.

As early as 1924, an airstrip for government and parcel carrier planes was established in St. George on the top of the Black Hill mesa. In 1940, a hangar was added, Dixie College offered an aeronautics course, and passenger flights to and from St. George began. In 1958, the runway was rebuilt and lengthened to support larger aircraft. The airport struggled financially until the late 1970s.

In the early 1960s, Dixie Airlines established passenger flights between Salt Lake City and the small St. George Municipal Airport with a roundtrip ticket costing $40. In 1972, Sid and Ralph Atkins bought the airline and changed the name to Skywest Airlines. The company struggled for the first few years, but by the mid-1980s, it became a Delta connection carrier with routes to 38 cities in eight states.

BIBLIOGRAPHY

Alder, Douglas D. and Karl F. Brooks. *A History of Washington County: From Isolation to Destination.* Salt Lake City, UT: Utah State Historical Society, 1996.

Archival Collections and Oral History Collections, Special Collections & Archives, Dixie State University.

Arrington, Leonard J. "The Mormon Cotton Mission in Southern Utah." *Pacific Historical Review* 25, No. 3 (August 1956): 221–238.

Bleak, James G. *Annals of the Southern Mission: A Record of the History of the Settlement of Southern Utah.* Edited by Aaron McArthur and Reid L. Neilson. Salt Lake City, UT: Greg Kofford Books, 2019.

Brooks, Juanita. "Utah's Dixie… The Cotton Mission." *Utah Historical Quarterly* 29, No. 3 (July 1961).

Dixie Journalist Chatter. St. George, UT: 1939–1952.

Dixie News. St. George, UT: 1922–1937.

Dixie Owl. St. George, UT: 1916–1921.

Dixie Sun. St. George, UT: 1952–2012.

Larson, Andrew Karl. *I Was Called to Dixie: The Virgin River Basin: Unique Experiences in Mormon Pioneering.* Salt Lake City, UT: Deseret News Press, 1961.

Miller, Albert E. *The Immortal Pioneers: Founders of City of St. George, Utah.* St. George, UT: self-published, 1946.

Revised Ordinances of the City of St. George. 1902, 1915, 1939.

Rio Virgin Times. St. George, UT: 1868–1869.

St. George. St. George, UT: 1878–1898.

Washington County News. St. George, UT: 1898–1988.

INDEX

Arizona Strip, 7, 8, 12, 25, 76, 100, 102, 104
Arrowhead Trail, 109–111, 116
Big Hand Cafe, 36, 82, 115
Bleak, James, 7, 9, 16
Booth, James J., 30, 70
Brooks, Juanita, 25
CCC, 37, 66, 83
cotton, 11, 22, 37, 63, 64, 66, 68
dam, 37, 63, 65, 72, 80, 83, 93, 96, 98
Dixie Academy, 32, 49
Dixie College, 18, 55, 60, 62, 109, 125
Dixie Normal College, 33–35, 54
Dodge's Spring, 71
Dominguez-Escalante Expedition, 7, 8, 12, 102
floods, 9, 11, 37, 43, 65, 80, 83, 85, 96, 97, 124
football, 61
Great Depression, 11, 36, 37, 54, 56–58, 73, 80, 83, 84, 95,
Honeymoon Trail, 99, 100, 102–104
Interstate 15, 8, 64, 99, 116, 123, 124
Lee, John D., 12, 15, 102
library, 16, 25, 51–53, 55, 62
McGregor Hospital, 23, 89
Morris, David, 18
Mountain Meadows, 9, 15, 25
Native Americans, 7–8, 14, 15, 21, 63, 69, 77, 102, 120
nuclear tests, 93, 120
oil, 74, 75, 89, 106
opera house, 28, 29, 35, 81
Paiutes, 7–8, 13, 63, 103
peaches, 63, 68, 94
Phoenix, Mary, 24
Pine Valley, 7, 9, 17, 20, 36, 43, 100
post office, 28, 68, 71, 78, 84
ranching, 63, 76, 77, 90, 92
Santa Clara River, 7, 8, 14, 37, 43, 65, 80, 83

Shivwits, 7, 8, 13, 21, 24, 37, 56
Silver Reef, 18, 73
Snow Canyon, 120–122
Snow, Erastus, 18, 28, 69
Snow, Leo A., 46, 49, 83, 106
social hall, 27–29, 43
Spanish Trail, 8, 9, 15
St. George Stake Academy, 16, 18, 31, 43, 47, 48, 50
St. George Elementary, 43, 57
sugar beets, 63, 64, 81
tabernacle, 21, 27, 30, 41, 43, 47, 55, 67, 68
temple, 20, 21, 27, 38, 79, 95, 99–101, 104, 105
tithing office, 16, 21, 63, 69
tourism, 2, 63, 96, 99, 109, 110, 115, 118
turkey, 63, 82, 85, 90, 91
Virgin River, 8, 11, 12, 16, 37, 63–66, 79, 80, 85, 95–99, 113, 123, 124
Washington County News, 70, 78
Whipple, Maurine, 26, 87
Woodward School, 24, 43, 45–47, 52, 53, 56, 57
World War I, 18, 31–33
World War II, 24, 38
Young, Brigham, 2, 7, 12, 15, 16, 64, 66, 99–101, 105
Zion National Park, 46, 109, 113–115

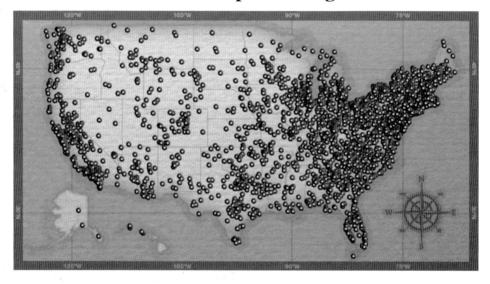